Best wishes to
Jocelyn & George –

Antony Hopkins

Antony Hopkins

DOWNBEAT MUSIC GUIDE

Illustrated by Marc

OXFORD UNIVERSITY PRESS

1977

London   Oxford   New York

Oxford University Press, Walton Street, Oxford OX2 6DP

Oxford, London, Glasgow, New York, Toronto, Melbourne, Wellington,
Cape Town, Ibadan, Nairobi, Dar es Salaam, Lusaka, Kuala Lumpur,
Singapore, Jakarta, Hong Kong, Tokyo, Delhi, Bombay, Calcutta,
Madras, Karachi

ISBN 0 19 311322 8

© Antony Hopkins and Mark Boxer 1977

The extract from Webern's *Three Songs* is reproduced by permission of
Universal Edition (London) Ltd

Designed by Malcolm Young MSIA MSTD
Filmset and printed in Great Britain by
BAS Printers Limited, Over Wallop, Hampshire
and bound by The Pitman Press, Bath

Prelude

If you like a good gripping story with a plot that keeps you guessing to the end, dictionaries of any sort make poor reading; the subject-matter changes too rapidly for coherence, the language tends to be stilted, the love-interest negligible. As the great Sir George Grove may have said (and who's to say he didn't?): 'A dictionary is no laughing matter.'

Feel relieved, then, that this is not a dictionary. It is a semi-serious look at a number of musical terms— ones which the untutored music lover may come across as he wades through the programme notes while the orchestra assembles, or as he mitigates the boredom of actually listening to a record by reading the backs of record-sleeves. I have omitted plenty of really obscure words—ones like 'gittern' (must be a bird, surely?), or 'aerophone' (in case of emergency dial *Conchord 999*), or 'dump' (dictionaries may be no laughing matter, but there's no need to pile on the depression). Here, though, are most of the words we ought to know, but whose exact meaning somehow escapes us, such as—well, read on, and you'll see.

In earlier times composers expected performers to put in embellishments and decorations. Sceptical of the present-day reader's ability to do this, I have gladly entrusted the task to Marc, whose ornamentation is stylish and impeccable; like an *appoggiatura* (q.v.) it is always on the beat.

[4]

A capella

To begin with a spelling mistake, this term should more properly be spelt with two ps (as in pianissimo), *A cappella*. The more cheerful variant *Alla cappella* is also acceptable, though it is erroneous to suppose that this is Italian for saying 'Hello' while raising one's cap. It is properly applied to unaccompanied church music (lit. 'In chapel') in which harmony is used; consequently it would not be used to describe plainsong, which is sung in unison, thus saving all the bother of copying out separate parts.

Occasionally instruments were employed to double the voice parts, whether for reasons of ostentation or because the choir's intonation was dodgy is not known. In such cases the term *A cappella* was also used, thus sowing doubt and confusion in the minds of those who look for unequivocal definitions.

Unaccompanied choral music, usually religious, is the generally accepted meaning.

Acciaccatura

(pron. A-*tchak*-atoora)   It has been suggested that this term came into existence during a rehearsal of Vivaldi's *The Seasons* when, reaching the movement called 'Winter', the leading violinist sneezed violently at the very moment he was about to play. Although the legend is discredited, it serves to remind us of the true meaning, derived from the Italian verb *acciaccare*, to crush, thus 'a crushed note'.

[5]

Strictly speaking an acciaccatura should be played simultaneously with the note against which it is crushed:

It thus provided a good excuse for thick-fingered noblemen who habitually played handfuls of wrong notes on early keyboard instruments. Nowadays the acciaccatura sign, a quaver printed in small type with its tail crossed out, ♪, indicates a note played as close as possible in time to the following note, but *before* the beat. (*See* APPOGGIATURA.)

Accidentals

Frequent occurrences in amateur music-making, especially when sight-reading. It is typical of the muddle-headed nature of musical notation that this term, with its implications of error, should be applied to notes that the composer is particularly anxious should *not* be misread. *Accidentals* are the symbols whereby the composer indicates notes foreign to the key of a piece; there are five, sharp(♯), double-sharp (×), flat (♭), double-flat (♭♭), and natural (♮). They precede all those notes that disturb the strict tonality of a composition, but since such notes are invariably put in by the composer on purpose it seems strange to describe them thus.

Accidentals contained within the key-signature, such as three sharps for A major, are called *essentials* (q.v.) since they are adhered to throughout the piece,

except when contradicted by an accidental natural—
on purpose of course.

Alberti bass

If you play a chord of three or four notes on the
piano it will gradually die no matter how hard you
press. It's frustrating, but there it is—or rather,
there it isn't any longer. One way of solving the
problem is simply to repeat the chord:

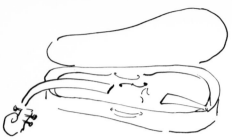

In the eighteenth century a minor composer called Domenico Alberti drew on the principles of artificial respiration as a way of keeping a chord alive, gently rocking it to and fro thus:

It was a great solution as long as you could think of a good enough tune to put above it. Alberti couldn't; Mozart and Haydn could.

Aleatory music

The earliest known crap-game was Aleae or dice, as played by the Ancient Romans. (Most of them were probably quite young at the time but it's not worth arguing about.) Little did they realize that their simple game would in the twentieth century become part of the daunting apparatus used by a certain, or perhaps uncertain, group of composers in their search for novelty. Once music had endured the rigor mortis of total serialization, in which all the elements, pitch, rhythm, and dynamics were plotted with mathematical inevitability, some reaction had to set in. How could one reintroduce the quality of surprise so brilliantly exploited by composers in earlier centuries?

One answer was to write music in sections which could be played in varying orders, the order being dictated by some such random device as throwing dice, drawing a card, dialling a girl-friend, or whatever fancy decreed. The odds on the work ever sounding the same twice thus become astronomical, and the composer gets the satisfaction of writing what appears to be a number of different works for no extra effort. Such music is described as aleatory.

Alla breve

Literally translated means 'in shortness', which shows why it is never literally translated. Basically it is an injunction to get a move on even though the music looks slow. In earlier periods of notation there was a tendency to use breves, semibreves, and minims where later composers would have used minims, crotchets, and quavers. The custom still exists in many a hymn-book and tends to have an inhibiting effect on tempo. As is usually the case, scholars disagree about the precise interpretation of *alla breve*; but the visual symbol ¢ indicates that the music should be performed twice as fast as it would be were the C not to be bisected. (In exceptional cases and in manuscripts only, it can also mean that he's crossed the damn thing out because it should be in $\frac{3}{4}$ after all, but this only occurs with composers who are unusually bad at counting.)

Amen

The final cadence at the end of a hymn, psalm, or prayer. The one that falls by a tone and the one that rises by a semitone are both perfect examples of perfect cadences:

The one that stays on the same note is an example of a plagal cadence:

so called because the organist finds it a plagal nuisance if the congregation sings a going-up-or-down one when he's playing a staying-on-the-spot one. In oratorio, masses, and the like, an excuse for composers to write very long fugues using only one word (e.g. 137 repetitions of Amen in the final chorus of *Messiah*).

Appoggiatura

(Ital: literally 'leaning', though not too heavily since early instruments were on the frail side)   A sort of slow-motion replay of an *acciaccatura* (q.v.), but *on*

Appoggiatura ...

A note that a performer lingers on...

the beat instead of just before it. A note that the
performer lingers on for expressive reasons, usually
in conflict with the supporting harmony. For this
reason it was printed in small type so as not to upset
the harmony teachers of the time. A phrase such as

could well have given an eighteenth-century Associated Board examiner a fit of the vapours. 'Print it

this way,' George Frideric or Wolfgang would say—

'it won't worry them so much; anyway there's always the chance they'll be so shortsighted they won't actually notice.'

Atonality

The state of being without a tonality. In classical music much importance was attached to the concept of tonality, the key in which a composition was largely conceived. We are all used to the idea of identifying a work by key, a sonata in A major, a symphony in C minor, etc. Such a label indicates the 'home' key from which the composer will start and to which with reasonable luck will ultimately return. Strictly speaking such labels are seldom accurate, and Beethoven's Fifth Symphony, for instance, should properly be described as 'Symphony No. 5 (well, it was called No. 6 at the first performance but don't be put off by that) in C minor with excursions into E♭ major, F minor, A♭ major, E♭ minor, G minor, G♭ major, B♭ minor, C♭ major (!), D♭ major, F♯ minor, G major, C major, F major, a slow movement in A major, a scherzo in C minor and C major, and a finale in C major'. Beethoven knew that if he put all that on the title-page the printers would be sure to get it wrong, and he'd have to keep on writing angry letters about it, so he settled for C minor as a reasonable compromise.

This shows that tonality was already a pretty shifty business even back in 1808. As the nineteenth century ground remorselessly onwards, introducing unhealthy influences such as Wagner and Tchaikovsky, so the entire concept of tonality became increasingly eroded. Critics attacked Wagner for his excessive use of chromatic harmony, harmony uncommitted to a specific key, failing to appreciate that (practical man of the theatre that he was) he knew the singers would be lost for much of the time, and that therefore it was only fair that the orchestra shouldn't know which key they were in either. At the beginning of the twentieth century the principle

of tonality finally collapsed; Debussy took refuge in the whole-tone scale which has neither beginning nor end, Schoenberg established the ultimate democratic principle that all twelve notes of the chromatic scale should have equal importance.

Atonal music is music without a home key, not 'in' D minor or whatever. But it is also music without *any* harmonious chords, because these would make the listener think that it *was* in a key. Tonal eclipse!—as Samson might have sung.

B.A.C.H.

Bachelor of Arts; Companion of Honour. Also a way of spelling out Bach's name in musical notation. According to English convention the notes of music are identified by the letters of the alphabet from A to G. Apart from minor confusions such as the fact that C can also be called B♯ or E be called F♭ the system is reasonably straightforward. But in logical Germany,

Bach ....

where everything is orderly and predictable, the note B♭ is called B and B♮ is known as H. This was presumably ordained by an early member of the Bach family as the only way he could spell his name on the keyboard.

Schumann, one of the more literate composers, spotted the further possibilities of German nomenclature, since E♭ is called Es (=S) and A♭ is called As. The so-called *Sphinxes* that appear in the middle of *Carnaval* spell respectively S C H A, As C H, and A S C H, the first being the nearest he could get to Schumann, and the other two being alternative musical spellings of the small town Asch where an early girl-friend lived.

In time composers got so carried away with the idea of translating words into musical notation that they continued up the keyboard taking H as the jumping-off point so that C became I, D became J, and so on. In this way Ravel could write an enchanting Menuet on the name of Haydn

a number of composers could write pieces on the name Fauré, though without any notably acute accents, while Shostakovich 'signed' a number of his works with the musical monogram D Es C H, for Dmitri SCHostakovich.

Bar

Where to find orchestral musicians whenever they are not actually playing. Also the upright lines drawn across the stave immediately before the primary rhythmic stress; however, such lines are more commonly called bar-lines, and the term bar may refer to the total music (or silence) contained between two bar-lines. In America the term 'measure' is used instead, probably because during Prohibition conductors didn't wish to make the players break down at the mention of the word 'bar' (see first definition).

Bémol

French for flat; not to be confused with appartement.

Bitonality

Music written so as to sound in two keys simultaneously. It may be in two clearly defined strands or in block harmonies, e.g.

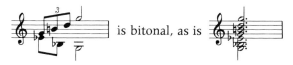 is bitonal, as is

Much used by composers such as Bartók, Holst, Milhaud, and Stravinsky, it is a way of making one's music seem more 'modern' than it really is. Mozart used it to comical effect in his 'Musical Joke' (K.522) but the others were usually pretty serious about it.

Bow

Traditional method of acknowledging applause. There are many variants, the disdainful nod of the head, the prolonged stoop forward, the supple sway, the hands clasped above the head. Also an inordinately expensive stick shaped in such a way that its opposite ends are joined together by horsehair whereby players of stringed instruments set the string in vibration and sustain the sound. Surprisingly the bow for a double bass is shorter than a violin's, perhaps because the bass-player has his hands full in more senses than one.

Broken chord

It is essential to spell this correctly, as 'broken cord' might lead to confusion with 'broken string', a frequent hazard for violinists and other players of stringed instruments, including aggressive pianists. A chord is said to be 'broken' when its component notes are played consecutively rather than together, e.g.

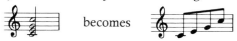

The posh word for this is *arpeggio*; but since the plural *arpeggios* sounds wrong, while the linguistically correct *arpeggii* is difficult to pronounce convincingly, 'broken chords' represents a cowardly British solution to a terminological problem.

Cadenza

The orchestra's favourite part of a solo concerto,
when they can get on with reading *Playboy, Autocar,*
etc. while the soloist sweats it out alone. Originally,

in solo instrumental or vocal music the final cadence (*see* AMEN) of a phrase or movement would be decorated by the performer at will, just to show he was every bit as important as the composer. In concertos it became the convention that towards the end of the first movement the orchestral part would build to a climax and then break off on a harmony known as a cadential six-four, the sort of odds laid on the soloist's chances of getting through the next bit without a mistake. The ensuing cadenza was supposedly improvised on the spur of the moment. Bitter experience taught composers the folly of letting soloists loose in this fashion (as when Melba interpolated variations on 'The Star-spangled Banner' into Rossini's *Barber of Seville*), and subsequently it became the normal practice for cadenzas to be as carefully composed as the rest of the work. By tradition they are supposed to be difficult to play, so that the soloist can show off his skills. Traditionally also they would end with a prolonged trill, the nearest musical equivalent to an alarm-clock, its purpose being to rouse the orchestra from slumber—the ones who have nothing to read, that is.

Canon

A form of music in which a tune is followed by its own shadow, an exact copy of the original line in most cases, though, like a shadow, it may be a lengthened (augmented) version of the initial melody or a shortened (diminished) version. One may also have inverted canons in which ascending intervals become descending ones and vice versa, canons cancrizans (lit. crab-like) which give the subject backwards, and canons in which the 'shadow' enters on a different degree of the scale. Canons were often presented as a form of musical puzzle, only a single line being given, the reader being challenged to discover how the line was to be 'canonized' against itself. The supreme example of such puzzle canons is to be found in the Musical Offering by J. S. Bach. Not to be confused with the ones required in the 1812 Overture which are spelt differently and which lack contrapuntal interest.

Chalumeau

As in 'Shall you mow the lawn or shall I?' A dark shady area of tone to be found in the lower register of the clarinet, similar to the 'chest-voice' of an alto but having one resonator instead of two.

Col legno

Effect discovered by Rossini* when a wooden-legged violinist put his foot in it by kicking his instrument. The pleasing twang of wood against gut caught the composer's fancy, but rather than cause the orchestra to undergo mass amputations, he hit (well-chosen word) upon the simpler solution of directing that

*Actually Mozart also used the effect in a Divertimento; however the title of the work 'Schlittenfahrt', has led to its suppression in polite society.

the music should be played 'Col Legno', with the wood of the bow, tapping the string with the bow held upside-down.

Coloratura

Surprisingly this is not an Italian word, being an English adaptation of the German *Koloratur*. What we mean by *coloratura* is actually *fioritura*, but this is harder to remember and less descriptive. *Coloratura* carries a nice suggestion of the scarlet-faced singer displaying prodigious vocal dexterity; it refers to a style of singing (usually allotted to a soprano voice) in which agility and the ability to scale the dizziest heights are the prime requisites. The Queen of the Night's arias in Mozart's *Magic Flute* are fine examples of the coloratura style at its best; Verdi was another master of the difficult art of providing vocal show-pieces that also had some musical substance. But there are innumerable examples of banal music in which the soprano is called upon to vie with a flute on the basis of 'anything-you-can-do-I-can-do-better'. The contest is invariably rigged in the singer's favour, which is unfair to flautists.

Concert pitch

Not as might be supposed a site for a pop festival, but an attempt to standardize the pitch to which instruments should be tuned. Over the last two hundred years pitch has risen substantially; the

screaming top As in the Choral Symphony would
have been a semitone lower in Beethoven's day;
Bach may well have heard his B minor Mass in what

concert pitch ...

we would call A minor. The measurement of pitch by establishing the number of vibrations or cycles per second shows that the note 'A' in the middle of the treble clef has been as high as 567·3 cycles per second or as low as 373·7. Handel's tuning fork gives us 422·5 as opposed to 440 cycles standardized today. In the mid-nineteenth century 435 was the norm. At the first performance of his piano concerto in B♭, Beethoven played the entire solo part up a semitone since the piano was so far below pitch that the orchestra couldn't tune down to its level. A lesser man would have burned the piano and claimed the insurance.

Continuo

In the days when composers knew that they would always be performing their works themselves, they would save time and trouble by writing a keyboard part consisting of a bass line only, using numerals as an accepted code to indicate the harmony; thus the figures $^6_4$—$^5_3$ would indicate that the 6th and 4th notes above the bass should descend to the 5th and 3rd notes. Hence the term 'figured bass'. This keyboard part, designed to hold things together 'continuously', was called the 'basso continuo' or just 'continuo'. The convention has emerged again in piano and guitar parts in jazz groups which may use a very similar notation. Possibly the basis for the widely held misconception that music and mathematics go together.

[25]

Counterpoint

The art of combining two or more lines of music in such a way that each has equal melodic interest, rather than several being subservient to one.

'Strict' counterpoint is an esoteric exercise designed to offer employment to a certain species of academic mind. Like the Ten Commandments it is almost entirely concerned with 'Thou Shalt Not'; it is the intellectual equivalent of the five-finger exercise. Palestrina is held to be the model on which all such exercises are based, a figure somewhat remote from the harsh facts of twentieth-century musical life. It is not so much in fashion nowadays; but in May 1911 a memorandum was issued by the Professors of Music of Oxford, London, Manchester, Dublin and Durham laying down twelve amendments to the strict rules of counterpoint that had obtained for centuries previously. It finished with the warning: 'It is not in our experience sufficiently borne in mind that anything in the nature of a "licence" should be used with reservation.' (see BAR.)

In creative and imaginative hands counterpoint can be profoundly satisfying and stimulating. The magisterial progress of a Bach organ fugue, the exhilaration of a Handel chorus, the sense of Homeric struggle in Beethoven's Grosse Fuge, the effortless integration of solo singers in a Mozart operatic ensemble—these are all examples of the delights of counterpoint for listener and performer alike. Obviously, though, it represents more of a challenge to the listener than simple melody since he needs to be able to follow several strands at once.

Crooks...

Crooks

Some would say agents and impresarios, but actually
an assortment of tubes of differing lengths by
which the player of the 'natural' horn (q.v.) in the
eighteenth and early nineteenth centuries could vary
its pitch. Without valves, the instrument could only
produce a limited number of notes known as the
harmonic series (q.v.). Thus one might have a horn
'in D' which could play the harmonic series in D
plus a few extra notes that a skilful player could
fake. To change it to a horn in F it wasn't necessary
to have another instrument; one simply pulled out
the D crook and stuck the F crook in its place, where-
upon one could play the harmonic series in F.

[27]

Da capo

Lit. 'from the head', or as the modern player would say 'from the top'. In the eighteenth century much value was placed on symmetry, balance in design. One of the most satisfying musical forms is what is popularly known as ABA; section A presents the main material, section B gives a contrast of mood and key, and then one repeats section A again *'Da Capo'*. In due course composers began to feel that this was a bit of a cheat; the simple *Da Capo* concept flowered into the more complete sonata form scheme of exposition, development, and recapitulation. The recapitulation could be said to be derived from the *Da Capo* convention.

Acceptable enough in oratorio, the *Da Capo* aria was deadly in opera, as Handel found to his cost. By going back to square one, the formula impeded the development of the plot. Audiences grew impatient of the hero who, loins girded for battle, could not bring himself to leave the stage simply because of a musical convention. Gilbert and Sullivan's famous line 'But damme you don't go' would have been fair critical comment.

Dal segno

An alternative to the above, but a short cut; go back not to the beginning but to the sign 𝄋 . Both *Da Capo* and *Dal Segno* were devised to save the composer copying out a lot of notes a second time.

Decoration

(also figuration)   The art of adding embellishments
to a melodic line. What with MS paper being so expensive, and sharpening quill pens wasting so much

Decoration ....

time, seventeenth- and eighteenth-century composers would often write down the bare outlines of a
tune, relying on the performer to pretty it up with
some tasteful twiddly bits. Mozart would be sur-
prised to hear present-day pianists solemnly playing
his slow movements exactly as written: whatever
else is right, this is certainly wrong.

Double stop

Term used in show-jumping to describe two refusals
at the same jump. Penalty: 6 faults; a third refusal
results in elimination. Also the technique of playing
two notes simultaneously on a stringed instrument
without using an open string. On a violin the open
or 'unstopped' strings are G, D, A, and E.

A chord like this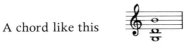

can therefore be played by 'stopping' or fingering
only one of its three notes. However, the two notes
B–G

would have to be played by putting one finger on
the A string, another on the E, hence double stopping. A four-note chord of G can easily be produced

[30]

by combining the two 'open' strings at the bottom with the two 'stopped' ones above

though the chord has to be spread slightly to allow for curvature of the bridge that supports the strings. By 'stopping' the two lower strings with one finger and using two more fingers on the upper strings the skilled player can play such a chord in other keys as well, e.g.

Sometimes all four fingers are called upon (as is frequently the case in guitar-playing). This is known as quadruple-stopping, and is to be avoided unless paid for at full soloist's rates.

Editing

The art of putting in the bits the composer left out, whether fingering, phrasing, tempo indications, dynamics (louds and softs), pedalling, even the notes themselves at times, plus the learned preface at the beginning saying how to interpret ornaments such as the Doppelschlag (double portion of cream) or the Pralltriller, not to mention how where and when the composer wrote the piece, his relationship with his employer Count Lasagne di Forno, his love for Bella Toblerone—all the helpful background stuff in fact which saves the performer from having to do any research of his own. The further back you go in musical history, the less thought composers seem to have given to posterity, little dreaming that three or four hundred years later one or two details of what they wrote might need explanation. Editors, musicologists, scholars, call them what you will, have done invaluable work in resurrecting early music, revising its notation so as to make it comprehensible to the modern performer, supplying correct harmonies in the continuo part (q.v.) for those incapable of doing it properly themselves, and encouraging a correct stylistic approach.

This sort of editing began in the nineteenth century. Editing then was often grossly misleading, bringing the music 'up to date' by an overlay of excessively dense harmony and superfluous expression marks. But credit for the initial spade-work must be given, the most noteworthy and historic example being the performance of Bach's St Matthew Passion promoted by the young Mendelssohn, which must have involved prodigious amounts of copying even to make the actual material. Twentieth-century scholarship has grown increasingly faithful to the original while also concerning itself with practicalities of performance.

For many years scholarly impact on concert performers was negligible, and to this day pianists will play such works as Bach's French Suites without observing any of the conventions Bach would have taken for granted, such as variants in the repeats, notes inégales (q.v.) and the like, let alone using an authentic instrument such as the harpsichord. However, the extraordinary renaissance of early instruments (or reconstructions thereof) and the availability of recorded performances that set a proper stylistic example, will in the long run have more effect than all the books in all the libraries in the world. (*See* MUSICA FICTA.)

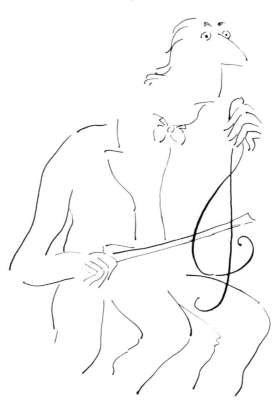

Embouchure

A good word to bandy about when you are talking to wind or brass players—'His embouchure doesn't seem quite right' always goes down well when discussing a rival performer; 'Did you have to change your embouchure at all?' when admiring a recently acquired clarinet. Avoid 'Have you read any good embouchures recently?' as it betrays ignorance. *Bouche* being the French for mouth, embouchure is literally the bit you put in your mouth, the mouthpiece. However, it is much more commonly used to describe the subtle relationship between the player's

Embouchure...

mouth and the instrument—exactly where one places the lips, tongue, and teeth in order to achieve the best possible control of tone and intonation. It is the nearest equivalent to 'touch' on the piano. The most remarkable and heroic instance of the surmounting of the problems of embouchure was when the world-famous oboist Leon Goossens suffered grave facial injuries in a car crash. Surgeons inserted more than sixty stitches in the region of his mouth, and many nerve-ends were severed, with a total loss of feeling as a result. Nevertheless Goossens taught himself to play again, and developed a completely new embouchure in the process.

Enharmonic

(usually in the expression *enharmonic change*)   The process, rather akin to a pun, whereby a note changes its harmonic significance by being notated differently. In acoustic theory there is a difference between B♯ and C known as the diesis (a ratio of 125:128, barely detectable). String players are able to reveal this difference, provided their use of vibrato doesn't obscure it altogether. The keyboard player has to accept that on the piano or organ B♯ and C are the same note. The musically ignorant might well ask why there should be two alternative notations for piano music; why bother with B♯ when C will do? The answer is that if the notes of the scale of C major in order are C D E F G A B C it is logical that the notes of C♯ major should be C♯ D♯ E♯ F♯ G♯ A♯ B♯ C♯. It would be irrational and confusing to the eye for such a scale to use any old notation that came to hand—C♯ E♭ F♮ F♯ A♭ A♯ C♮ D♭. The *sound* would be the same (on a piano, not on a violin), the notation chaotic.

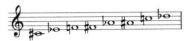

However, the situation can arise when, by the punning process I have suggested, the note B♯ might be used as a pivot to switch the harmony to C major thus:

This switch of notation is called an enharmonic change.

French composers, who are grammatically very correct, are particularly prone to maddeningly obfuscating notation; one of my favourite examples is the chord in Ravel,

which on closer examination turns out to be F major. In such cases one feels the rules might well be bent a little; a sort of temporary enharmonic change would be welcome even if ungrammatical.

Equal temperament

One might misconstrue this term as referring to the type of performer whose emotions are untouched by

[36]

whatever music he happens to be playing. Such players maintain a stoic indifference to the exhortations, cajoling, or even frenzy of conductors and tend to lurk in the back desks of the strings, where they can remain unnoticed as they placidly endure the tumult of Tchaikovsky or the battering of Berlioz. More usually the term *Equal Temperament* is employed to describe the revised system of tuning keyboard instruments brought about in Bach's time. (Hence the title 'Well-tempered Keyboard' for the Forty-eight Preludes and Fugues.) In the previous entry on *Enharmonic* change we have seen that by 'just' or exact intonation B♯ and C are not the same. In theory one can tune a keyboard instrument in such a way that it is exactly in tune according to acoustic laws; however, it will then only be in tune in a limited number of keys. For example if it is in tune in a 'sharp' key such as E major, the major third of the scale, G♯, is a critical note in establishing the tonality of E. If one then modulates to F minor, the G♯ will theoretically become an A♭ (enharmonic change) and will consequently sound out of tune. If you reverse the process and 'tune' your keyboard to the scale of A♭ major, you can modulate safely to F minor, for A♭ is common to both keys; however, you cannot modulate to E major because your A♭ then has to be thought of as a G♯ and it cannot change its adjustment, which is why to this day strings and piano can be an uneasy mixture. The system of *Equal Temperament* is a compromise by which the octave is divided into twelve practically equal semitones, the third, fourth, sixth, and seventh notes of the scale being tuned slightly sharp, the second

and fifth slightly flat. Bach wrote the two books of
Twenty-four Preludes and Fugues (there being
twelve major and twelve minor keys) to demonstrate
that the invention of Equal Temperament tuning had
made it possible to play in all keys on one instrument, though preferably not at the same time. That
came later . . .

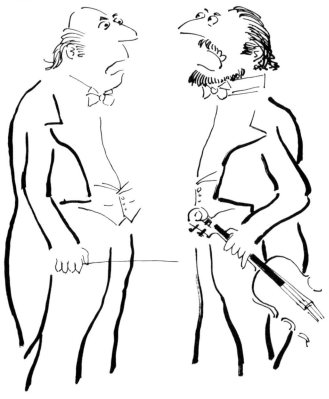

Equal temperament

Essentials

Like a number of compositions, this could be interpreted in many different ways. Essentials for organists include thin-soled shoes and trousers that are not too tight; essentials for guitarists are long thumb nails; harpists must have two feet, though pianists have been know to manage with only one hand. In fact the term in its technical sense is little used but is the proper name for those sharps or flats included in the key signature at the beginning of a composition. Hence the word 'accidentals' (q.v.) to describe other sharp or flat notes.

A few brave souls have tried to break the absurd academic restriction by which it is forbidden to mix flats and sharps in the same key signature. The proper key signature for G minor is two flats:

But since the F is usually sharpened it would seem both logical and practical to include it in the list of *essentials*.

There have also been instances of composers, Bartók and Hindemith among them, 'inventing' key signatures for practical convenience, e.g.

But these are few and far between.

False relations

Musical history is littered with family problems; Beethoven's nephew, Tchaikovsky's wife, Wagner's wives—or to be more accurate his friends' wives. Nevertheless, tempting though it is to dwell on these much more interesting matters, conscience compels me to concentrate on a more proper (in every sense) definition. Back in the Golden Days of the Elizabethan madrigalists, and even earlier, before composers had been got at by harmony teachers, it was quite acceptable to give a bit of spice to the harmony by mingling contradictory notes within the same chord. For instance, if you wanted to describe graphically the pain caused by your loved one's 'sharp disdain', you could impart a positive twinge to the word 'sharp' by harmonies such as these:

If the sharp and natural do not clash simultaneously, but one follows the other, that is a *false relation*, as here:

where the bass has been tactless enough to substitute an F♯ for the alto's F♮.

Much as the Church has been forced to adopt a more liberal attitude towards divorce, so critical opinion had to modify its feelings about false relations when William Walton exploited them to memorable effect in his viola concerto. (Published by O.U.P. Scores available at a price.)

Fortepiano

Early version of the piano in which, not surprisingly, they got everything the wrong way round, including the name; even the keys were the wrong colour, what we call the white notes being black and vice versa. Like the earliest horseless carriage, though, it represented a big breakthrough in instrumental technology. The strings, instead of being plucked as in the harpsichord, or pressed as in the clavichord, were struck by leather-coated hammers producing a pleasantly silvery tone. The name 'fortepiano' (loud-soft) drew attention to its prime advantage over its predecessors, the ability to vary the volume of sound by using greater or lesser force on the keys. (You can do this on the clavichord too, but it is so quiet that only one person at a time can hear it.) It was for this reason that the music of early composers for fortepiano such as C. P. E. Bach is littered with accents, and very frequently alternations between f and p. An entire generation of keyboard players had to be encouraged to change the habits of a lifetime and learn a new approach. Even in mature Mozart one can find evidence of this when he goes

so far as to mark each note of a brief scale passage
with alternating dynamics.

Nobody seems to know why the name *Fortepiano*
was reversed to *Pianoforte*, though the earliest form
of piano invented by Cristofori in the first quarter of
the eighteenth century was called a *gravicembalo col
piano e forte*. It is possible that stressing the *forte*
aspect might have alarmed potential buyers with
sensitive ears, and that pianoforte could thus be
described as a 'soft sell'.

Fugue

In psychology, a state of changing consciousness often combined with a sudden impulse to wander away—something not unknown amongst audiences faced with the prospect of hearing fugues. One of the stricter musical forms, fugues have the reputation of being academic and boring, which, in the minds of less inspired composers, they often are. A fugue may be in two or more parts; it will begin with a statement of the subject in a single part or voice, which will then be taken over by the second voice while the first part continues with the *countersubject*; in due course part number three will enter with the *subject* while part two takes over the *countersubject*. Anything irrelevant to the subject is known as an *episode* for want of a better definition. When the subject overlaps itself it is known as a *stretto*. Subjects may also be *augmented* (notes twice as long) or *diminished* (notes twice as short); they may also be *inverted* without any loss of dignity. While Bach was the greatest master of fugal composition, fugues can crop up in the most unlikely places such as the Witches' Sabbath in the Fantastic Symphony of Berlioz, and the Finale of Walton's First Symphony. The very people who proclaim intense dislike of fugues are likely to adore Handel's *Messiah*, many of whose choruses are fugal.

There is an old saying that fugues are the type of music in which the voices come in one by one while the audience goes out one by one but there is no statistical evidence to support this; audiences have been known to leave in droves.

Furniture

(also Fourniture: Fr.)   Unbelievably, a stop on the organ, corresponding to the Mixture (q.v.). Organ stops have a variety of names showing an almost poetic fantasy; among these may be listed, in no particular order save that dictated by affection, Clarabella, Dulciana, Vox angelica (as opposed to Vox humana), Keraulophon, Unda maris, Lieblich gedackt, Hohl flute, Gemshorn, and Echo gamba. (Not to be confused with 'Ecco – gamba!' as whispered lecherously by one Italian orchestral player to the other when an operatic soprano ventures too near to the edge of the stage.)

Ground

(often coupled with bass, *ground bass*)   A form of
which Purcell was one of the greatest masters;
briefly it is a composition in which the same phrase
in the bass is repeated a number of times without
alteration, while above it the composer extends an
expressive melodic line often richly harmonized.
The skill lies in the inventiveness the composer
displays in escaping from the potentially inhibiting
effect of the reiterated bass—hence the phrase 'getting off the ground'. It is particularly apposite that
one of the finest examples of a ground should be
'When I am laid in earth' from *Dido and Aeneas*.
When the composer cheats by introducing variations
of rhythm and by allowing the repeated theme to
rise out of the bass, it becomes a passacaglia (q.v.).

Grupetto

Small Italian pop group, idolized by teeni-bopperini;
also a group of ornamental notes such as a turn.

Hackamore

A bitless bridle for a horse that has difficulty with
its embouchure. It doesn't really belong in a musical
dictionary but is put in as a bonus; useful word in
Scrabble.

Harmonics

The tonal equivalent of the spectrum. Just as white light passed through a prism may be shown to consist of a number of different coloured bands, so individual notes are made up of a compound of sounds whose varying predominance causes the differences of timbre associated with differing instruments. The note sounded is called the fundamental, while all the components above the fundamental are known as 'upper partials' or 'overtones'. These overtones fall tidily into a series of steadily diminishing intervals whose relationship to one another may be established by neat mathematical principles, e.g.

Fundamental

Taking the fundamental as 1, the remaining fractions are $\frac{1}{2} \frac{1}{3} \frac{1}{4} \frac{1}{5} \frac{1}{6} \frac{1}{7} \frac{1}{8} \frac{1}{9} \frac{1}{10} \frac{1}{11} \frac{1}{12} \frac{1}{13} \frac{1}{14} \frac{1}{15} \frac{1}{16}$ and so on (by ever diminishing intervals) up to infinity. (The upper notes are only of interest to bats and highly trained dogs.)

The pitch of these overtones as written on the stave is only an approximation beyond the fraction of $\frac{1}{11}$. As a practical demonstration of this, listen to the horn solo at the start and finish of Britten's *Serenade* for tenor, horn, and strings; it is played as if on the 'open' or 'natural' horn (q.v.) using only the notes of the harmonic series, and consequently sounds partially 'out of tune' to the uninitiated ear.

On string instruments, harmonics are frequently used as an effective way of producing high notes. Touch the string lightly at the halfway mark and it will sound an octave higher; touch it one third of its length along and you will produce a note an octave and a fifth higher. There are five such natural harmonics to be found on each string, equivalent to the fractions $\frac{1}{2}-\frac{1}{6}$ in the above table. In addition, the skilled player can produce artificial harmonics in which the string is firmly stopped with one finger while being lightly touched at a suitable higher point with another finger (preferably his own).

In effect, the firmly-stopping finger is simply shortening the string, thereby raising its pitch, while the light-touch finger finds a point a quarter of the way along the now shortened string, producing a sound two octaves above the fundamental or 'fingered' note. Such artificial harmonics are written with a hollow diamond-head a fourth above the stopped or fingered note.

Harmonics are as basic to music as genes and hormones are to biology; however, the average listener is only likely to be aware of them in music for string instruments, which includes harp and guitar as well as the violin family. Their effect is fluty and ethereal. Stravinsky uses harmonic glissandi magically near the beginning of *Firebird*.

Idée fixe

(Fr.) Persistent refusal of French music students
to correct mistakes as when Debussy's harmony
teacher found his cadences far from perfect. More
properly used to describe a theme or motif that appears in more than one movement of a symphonic
work, thus helping to create a sense of unity, albeit
sometimes at a rather superficial level. Anticipated
by Haydn in his Symphony no. 46 and by Beethoven
in his Fifth Symphony (where a 'memory' of the
scherzo makes a notable reappearance in the finale) it
became very much the vogue during the nineteenth
century when composers began to feel the need
to counter the tendency for large-scale works to
become somewhat unmanageable. To take a 'fixed

idea' that could recur in all movements of a work—
or at least the first and last movements—seemed a
valid solution to the problem, especially for those
works that had a programmatic as well as a symphonic basis. Notable examples include Schubert's
Wanderer Fantasy (where the link is only per-
functory), Berlioz's Symphonie Fantastique, Liszt's
Faust Symphony and Piano Sonata, César Franck's
Symphony and Violin Sonata, Tchaikovsky's Fourth
and Fifth Symphonies, and Elgar's First Symphony.
The Wagnerian 'leitmotiv' (q.v.), a theme associated
with one character or object throughout an opera, is
an extension of the *idée fixe* concept.

Indeterminacy

Somewhat as a painter such as Jackson Pollock can
become fascinated with the random patterns produced by rivulets and splashes of paint, so the indeterminate composer explores the possibilities of
mingling musical sounds of varying tempo and pitch
in such a way as to produce a seemingly haphazard
effect. Indeterminacy seems to have evolved as a
protest against the theory of total serialization, in
which every musical element was planned with an
inflexibility that soon proved unacceptable. To
describe it as spontaneous improvisation would be
misleading; a New Orleans jazz group improvise
spontaneously, but they aim to fit into an agreed
sequence of harmonies. The composer using indeterminate methods seeks to produce, by chance,

combinations of sound that are too free to trap by any normal system of notation.

The usual technique is to specify certain basic shapes on which the players are then expected to improvise until a given sign, at which point they will move on to the next section. Cynics might argue that it is an evasion of responsibility on the part of the composer, yet it has sometimes shown itself to be an effective device. Haydn might have welcomed it when writing the 'Representation of Chaos' at the start of *The Creation*.

While amateurs have known all about indeterminacy in the field of pitch for centuries, it has only recently become respectable among professionals. Composers such as Penderecki often use visual symbols involving no conventional notation; orchestral players usually describe such approximations to pitch as 'playing naturally'.

Interrupted cadence

A method of putting off the inevitable. If a perfect cadence can be described as an Amen (q.v.), an *interrupted* cadence, with its inability to finish a phrase before going on to something else, might be described as an 'Ah—women!' Technically, it is a way of producing an element of surprise; the composer prepares the way for a perfect cadence, which has a sense of finality, but then interpolates an unexpected chord, thereby 'interrupting' the cadence.

Interval

Welcome respite during lengthy concerts during which members of the audience can ensure that they are seen by the 'right' people. American intervals are longer, being called Intermissions (no ecumenical implication). Also the difference in pitch between any two sounds, measured in a typically confusing way by a mixture of numerical and alphabetical concepts. Intervals are counted from the lower note upwards, and are classified according to the number of degrees of the stave, i.e. the alphabetical letter, not the number of tones or semitones contained therein. Thus C–A♭ is a 6th (C D E F G A) while C–G♯ is a 5th (C D E F G), albeit one is minor and the other augmented. (Their sound on a keyboard is identical, as is the number of semitones, eight.) Elements of the class system show in the naming of intervals: 4ths, 5ths, and 8ves represent the higher order in so far as they are called 'perfect'; 2nds, 3rds, 6ths, and 7ths are major or minor; 4ths can also be augmented, 5ths can be augmented or diminished, and 7ths can be diminished. 2nds, 7ths, and all augmented or diminished intervals are social outcasts, discords.

[51]

One of the commonest chords in music, the diminished seventh, has its outer extremities a major 6th apart, but never say so in academic circles or you will be ostracized.

Inversion

A word that has several meanings in music, most of them confusing. Since intervals (q.v.) are always calculated from the lower note, if you invert an interval you have to change its name. Thus the interval of a 2nd

when inverted becomes a 7th

Perfect intervals remain perfect even when they are subjected to the indignity of being turned upside-down; 5ths become 4ths and vice versa. In harmony, a chord spaced in such a way as *not* to have its root in the lowest part is said to be an inversion, even though it may be higher than the so-called 'root position', e.g.

In themes, usually in fugal subjects, inversion means a sort of mirror image whereby ascending intervals become descending ones, etc. Inversion is also one of the processes a 12-note series has to suffer (*see* SERIALISM). A pedal-point (q.v.) that has lost its way sufficiently to find itself at the top of the music instead of the bottom is known as an inverted pedal point, but not often.

Jam-nuts

I had to include these as they sound so tasty. Actually part of a device patented by the American piano maker Gertz in 1900 known as a 'tension-resonator', by which, with the aid of tie-rods, jam-nuts, and a central dished ring with a screwbolt inserted in its centre, the soundboard could be re-tensioned. Now you know.

Kapellmeister

(Ger: lit. Chapel-master)   A director of musical activities, not necessarily in a church; he might be employed in a theatre or a royal household. The Kapellmeister who *was* attached to a church might be responsible for choral and instrumental music and have an organist as his junior. Wherever he was, he would be expected to compose as much as perform. Haydn was a *Kapellmeister* for most of his life (Bach was not *Kapellmeister* at Leipzig but *Cantor,* a slightly different position).

The term *Kapellmeistermusik* came to have derogatory implications since the music written by a sort of musical equivalent to the Civil Service tended to lack inspiration. In German the word *Kapelle* has completely escaped from its ecclesiastical associations:

[53]

Jack Hylton's Band was once advertised as Jack Hylton's Kapelle to the surprise of the players.

Leitmotiv

(Ger. =leading motive)   Term devised by Wagner to describe a theme associated with a character or object throughout an opera, or indeed four operas in the case of the Ring cycle. Cynics might feel Heavy-motiv a more suitable term, and there is of course a danger that on hearing Siegfried's theme for the ump-teenth time as he stands expectant in the wings, the listener may react by saying 'Oh, not him *again*!' But in fact, as a musical device it was a brilliant solution to the problem of giving some overall unity and sense of symphonic development to the vast fabric of the operas. (*See* IDÉE FIXE.)

Madrigal

I have it on excellent authority that a telediphone
typist, transcribing an unscripted BBC programme,
consistently reproduced this word as Mad Wriggle.
The idea is charming but misleading. The *madrigal* is
a form of unaccompanied secular vocal composition.
In England it came to full flower in Elizabethan
times, though its origins were Italian and substantially earlier. The music tends to follow closely
the sentiments of the words. It is rhythmically free,
and shows skills in counterpoint, especially in imit-
ation between the voices. The words might be written by the composer himself and sometimes show
high poetic quality. Madrigals are much subject to
editing (q.v.).

A lighter form of madrigal known as a ballet or 'Fa
la' will use these syllables in an almost instrumental
way as a conclusion to each verse.

Minnesinger

Neither a singer less than five feet tall, nor even one
with a virtually inaudible voice. Minnesingers were
German troubadours of the 12th and 13th centuries,
give or take a hundred years. Presumably by the
processes of natural evolution they ultimately
became Meistersingers and we all know what hap-
pened to them.

[55]

Mixture

A type of organ-stop which enables the depression of a single key or note to produce a blend of sound from several pipes. These pipes reinforce the natural harmonics (q.v.) of the originating note, and thereby add an element of brightness which changes the tone colour in a way unique to the organ. It need not necessarily be disparaging then when one organist remarks about another's performance, 'Typical of old Wynnd-Blower, the same old mixture as before'— though it probably is. Disparaging I mean. (*See also* MUTATION.)

Modes

It was the pianist Eileen Joyce who gave new life to the word modes when she wore dresses chosen specifically to go with the mood of the music she was playing. Up until then it had referred exclusively to the formation of the scales on which ecclesiastical plainsong was founded. In theory there are fourteen such modes, each with a name derived from the Greek, such as Dorian, Phrygian, Lydian, Hypo-Mixo-Lydian, etc. However, two of the fourteen, the Locrian and the Hypo-Locrian, are only Hypo-thetical and do not actually exist. The modern scale of C major is identical with the Ionian mode (incidentally known as the 'Modus lascivus', the 'Wanton Mode'), while the scale of A minor is the Aeolian mode; these are the only two which are in contemporary use, hence 'C and A Modes'—which brings us back to Eileen Joyce.

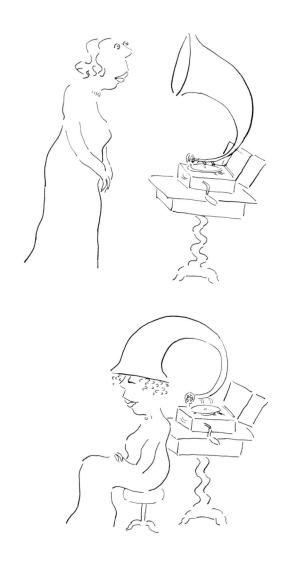

Mordent

From the Italian 'mordente' = biting. One of the most important musical ornaments, designed to give 'bite' to a note by a sharp reiterated attack, thus:

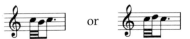

The early English term for these and other similar types of ornament was 'relish', which like 'biting' seems to have gastronomical connotations. 'Relish' admirably conveys the function of such ornamentation which was designed to draw attention to a note, since accentuation in terms of volume was not practicable on early keyboard instruments. The symbol for a mordent rising to the note above is ᴧᴠ ; a short line bisecting it, ᴧᴠ , indicates that the lower note should be employed. (The German for a lower mordent is *Pralltriller*.) There is also the *long mordent* in which four decorative notes are used instead of two.

Motet

Just as early instrumental music could be divided into the Sonata da Chiesa (Church Sonata) and the Sonata da Camera (Chamber or Room Sonata), so— at least in the sixteenth century—unaccompanied choral music could be classified as the Motet (sacred) or the Madrigal (q.v.) (secular). The Motet as a distinct musical form emerged way back in the thirteenth century. It was usually in three parts: the *tenor* (bass to us) sang phrases of plainsong very, very slowly; the *motetus*, the middle part, moved faster; and the *triplum* (treble to us—yes, it's the same word) faster still. The fact that the three parts often had different words, thereby making the text unintelligible, was not regarded as a hindrance, since cathedral acoustics are such that you can't hear the words anyway. However, only a couple of hundred years later more consideration was given to the text, although the contrapuntal nature of the composition still led to a more confused texture than that conveyed by the unisons of plainsong. By then—the fifteenth and sixteenth centuries—motets were in four or more parts in what to us is the normal style of part-writing. The English word 'anthem' refers to our local form of motet.

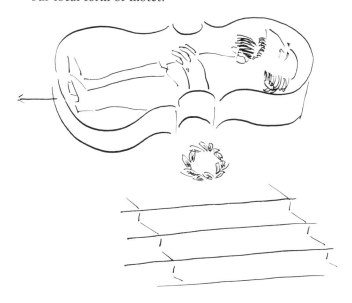

Musica ficta

One of the nicer problems in editing early music is
the insertion of accidentals (q.v.) into texts where
they have been omitted, either through carelessness,
or more frequently because the composer assumed the
performers would be aware of conventions that have
now long fallen out of use. 'Music is called *ficta*
when we make a tone to be a semitone, or, conversely,
a semitone to be a tone.' This unhelpful rule was
propounded in *Ars Contrapuncti*, a textbook of the
fourteenth century. Composers of the time were repre-
hensibly casual in their approach to such matters, and
since their musical habits were notably different from
ours, it is not surprising that performers of today need
guidance. Take a cadence like this:

Should the C be natural or sharp? In the eighteenth
century, C♮ would be unthinkable; in the fifteenth
century, it would probably have been C♯ if followed
by a chord of D *minor*, C♮ if followed by a chord of
D *major*. But since the sharp on F might well have
been omitted too, one still has a considerable area for
dispute. Singers and instrumentalists were expected to
know such things by instinct, and the original term
for 'accidental', *signum asininum* or 'ass's mark',
shows the contempt felt for anyone without the
musical sense to do the right thing without help.
Small wonder that the term 'accidentals' crept in,
when the performer's path was so hazardous. To

sum up, in a reputable edition of early music (such as those published by O.U.P.) the accidentals printed in small type are *Musica Ficta*.

Mutations

Despite the sinister connotations of this word in the realms of Science Fiction, in the context of music it refers to a type of organ stop. If a pianist plays the note middle C, he has a reasonable expectation that that is what he'll hear, assuming that the instrument is not defective or hopelessly out of tune. However, on the harpsichord or organ, the same middle C can be made to sound an octave lower by employing what is called a 16 ft. registration and an octave higher by using a 4 ft. registration. By the use of couplers one can even sound all three Cs while still only using the one finger, which makes octave-playing a lot easier. *Mutations* are an extension of this idea, adding a note other than those at an octave or two octaves' distance, for instance a fifth or an octave-and-a-fifth above the key actually depressed. The result, to an unindoctrinated ear, can sound like a rash of consecutive parallel fifths, something which the conventional harmony teacher would regard as outrageous. Like the Almighty, though, organists move in a mysterious way,* and they find the parallel motion induced by mutation stops quite acceptable.

*It is a fact that the Inland Revenue allow organists more pairs of trousers per annum than any other profession, on account of all the sliding about they have to do.

Natural horn

The original horn as used in Mozart's day and earlier, more or less similar in shape to the modern French horn but without any valves. Basically a simple conical brass tube, opening into a bell at the end furthest from the mouthpiece. Being over seven feet in length, it was somewhat impractical in a straight form, especially as it was originally an instrument of the chase—few horses would appreciate the instrument being rested on their heads or blown close to their ears. Forming the tube into a spiral coil solved the problem, with the additional advantage that the huntsman could then sling it over his shoulder.

The first refinement to be added was a tuning-slide that enabled the player slightly to adjust the pitch by lengthening or shortening the tube to a limited degree. From this was developed the idea of crooks (q.v.). These in turn were replaced by valves, which can divert the vibrating column of air into channels of different lengths (*see also* HARMONICS). Thereafter the horn was no longer natural.

Neumes

(also neums, pneums)   Early form of musical notation as used in plainsong during the Middle Ages and even earlier. To begin with, any sign such as ╱ or ╲ which reminded the singer which direction the melody went in. Later—and in some church music right up to the present day—the music was written on a four-line stave, the pitch being shown by block-like symbols, ╻ , ▬ and ◆ . Different durations were also indicated by coloration, a red note being a subdivision of a black. Subsequently hollow black notes replaced red, presumably to save the writer's time or possibly due to the difficulty of distinguishing black from red by candlelight. Considering the conditions they worked in, it's surprising the monks weren't blind, let alone colour-blind.

The whole subject of the notation of plainsong is fraught with numerous ambiguities and uncertainties. Neumes are grouped together in small clusters of notes, rather as quavers may be joined by a cross-bar. ⁏ ╲ ♪ ♥ are the most commonly found of such groups. For the devotee of plainsong, a visit to Solesmes to hear it sung to perfection might be described as a vision of neumatic bliss.

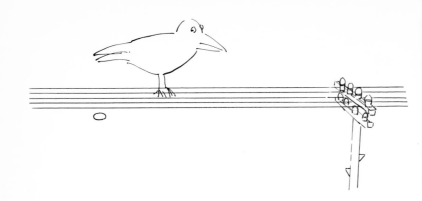

Notes inégales

(Fr. = unequal notes)   The most common method
of playing scales, runs, etc., especially amongst
amateurs. This is not as frivolous a definition as it
sounds, since in the early days of keyboard
playing the fingering of a two-octave scale was
2 3 2 3 2 3 2 3 2 3 2 3 2 3 2 3 4. The result can be imagined,
and composers were practical enough to realize that
the chances of getting equality and evenness in a
scale were so remote as to be hardly worth considering. Thus Frescobaldi in the Preface to his Toccatas
(1614) instructs the player to perform running pas-
sages written in equal quavers in uneven pairs,
the first note to be *shorter* than the second. In due
course necessity became the mother of convention,
and in eighteenth-century France in particular the
custom of *Notes Inégales* became synonymous with

good style. It was as though an epidemic of appoggiaturas (q.v.) had broken out, for now the first note of each pair was *lengthened*, producing a lilting rhythm described as *'louré'*. (This inequality only applied to groups of four or two notes, never to triplets, nor in rapid movements.) The official reason for *notes inégales* was that they added to the expressive character of the music. Much of seventeenth- and eighteenth-century rhythmic notation is ambiguous and today needs specialists to work it out. But vitality *is* imparted to the music by properly observing unwritten conventions. (*See also* EDITING.)

Obbligato

Another curiosity of musical nomenclature. It is derived from the Italian word for 'obligatory'; yet it normally means a decorative line, like a descant in a hymn or carol (though usually more elaborate) and so is quite optional. The oboe part in Bach's setting of 'Jesu, Joy of Man's Desiring'—once unforgettably introduced by a Radio 3 announcer as 'Jesu, Man of Joy's Desiring'—with its continuous undulating pattern of triplets is an *obbligato*. In works like Bach's *St Matthew Passion* each solo aria will tend to have a decorative obbligato on one or sometimes two solo instruments—a violin, an oboe, a viola da gamba, a pair of oboi d'amore—thereby giving it an individual timbre. The convention virtually died out during the nineteenth century. General orchestral standards improved then, and perhaps the word came into use not so much to describe the music as to remind the Kapellmeister (q.v.) that a first-class flautist, oboist, horn-player, or whatever was necessary (*obbligato*) before a performance could be contemplated.

Organum

This probably has nothing to do with organ-playing, though some say that it comes from 'organize' meaning 'make a sound like an organ'. It is the earliest western form of singing in harmony, dating roughly from the tenth century. Its most easily recognizable feature in its early stages is a tendency to move in strict parallel motion, in either fourths or fifths, like this:

Tu Pa - tris sem - pi - ter - nus es Fi - li - us.

Or it could start at a unison, wander apart to a fourth or fifth and wander back again, like this:

Rex cae - li, Do - mi - ne ma - ris un - di - so - ni,
Ti - ta - nis ni - ti - di squa - li - di - que so - li.

(It is ironic that centuries later, consecutive or parallel fifths were as strictly forbidden in harmony exercises as split infinitives in prose.)

Composers are always adventurous, and after a mere three hundred years we find 'organum' used to describe something different. A gregorian chant is sung very slowly: this is called the Tenor part (Latin 'tenere' = to hold). Above it is another part—or two, or even three—singing short quick notes. There may be twenty or even thirty notes in the upper parts to one in the tenor. Since we would call the tenor the bass, and in any case it is undemocratic to give one part so much less work to do than the other, all this is perhaps better forgotten (*See* MOTET.)

Ornaments

Signed photograph of Auntie Muriel, small plaster busts of Bach, or pottery souvenirs of Salzburg, as displayed on the tops of unused pianos. Also the name for any forms of embellishment by which a basic note in a melody (the *Principal*) has subsidiary notes added before or after it. For reasons elaborated elsewhere (see APPOGGIATURA, EDITING, MORDENT early composers left a great deal to the performer's inventiveness. They expected him to introduce decorations which might be simple or might transform the outline on the score into a fantastically ornamented structure. For instance, a phrase such as this:

might legitimately have been interpreted as:

Such ornamentation, superimposed by the player at his discretion, was not indicated on the score by written symbols.

But frequently the composer did indicate by a visual code precisely what additional notes he wished to be played. The proper interpretation of this code has been the subject of innumerable essays and textbooks, many written by the composers themselves (Morley, Frescobaldi, Quantz, C. P. E. Bach, Marpurg, etc., etc.). Even so there is still disagreement about how to interpret some of the many symbols used. Most of the differences arise from the fact that practices differed between one country or period and another. But even within one period, something like the tempo of a piece can affect the interpretation of an ornament.

Ornamentation in early keyboard music was partly a necessity brought about by the lack of sustaining power in the instruments themselves. But the elaborate decoration to be found equally in vocal and string music shows that its prime function was expressive rather than mechanical.

The practice of ornamentation continued into the nineteenth century, notably in music for solo piano—Chopin and Liszt—and in opera—Bellini, Donizetti, and Verdi. But composers virtually abandoned the shorthand symbols of earlier times (apart from the trill *tr* ---) in favour of more exact notation. Today the spontaneous ornamentation that Corelli or Vivaldi would have taken as a matter of course has largely died out of 'serious' music. Instead, its nearest equivalent is to be found in the gifted hands of jazz instrumentalists.

Ostinato

(lit. It. = obstinate)   A musical phrase repeated identically a number of times. A well-known trick amongst orchestral players who lose their place is to jump three lines and play the same bar over and over again *until it fits*; then press on with the general throng. This, however, is different from the composed ostinato. Here the composer deliberately repeats a phrase, either as a primitive way of working up excitement (e.g. rock 'n' roll) or as a means of demonstrating his skill in avoiding monotony despite the use of potentially monotonous material. A ground bass (q.v.) is one kind of ostinato, but only one kind. For instance an ostinato may appear in any part; it may be rhythmic; it may be a sequence of harmonies. Perhaps the most famous example of a

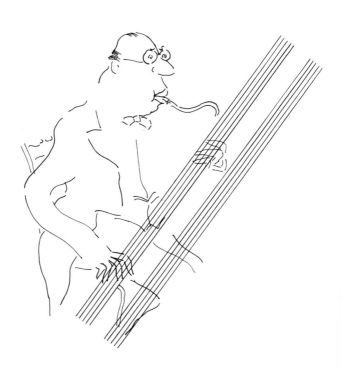

sustained ostinato is Ravel's *Bolero*—which is not actually a Bolero at all, the title being intended for a ballet—in which the same two-bar figure is repeated 169 times.

Stravinsky was a notable exploiter of the effect, while contemporary composers of 'indeterminate' music (q.v.) often indicate a figure that should be played over and over again in free tempo until a sign is given to move on to the next pattern.

Palindrome

It was once unkindly said of Reger that the only thing to be said in his favour was that his name was a *palindrome*, i.e. that it spelt the same backwards or forwards. As a musical form the palindrome is too complicated to occur often. There are a number of sixteenth-, seventeenth-, and eighteenth-century examples to be found, especially amongst the canons (q.v.), often written as an intellectual diversion, a musical equivalent of the crossword-puzzle. Examples of a musical palindrome are to be found in Bach's Musical Offering, in a Scherzetto by Mozart, and most notably in the Prelude and Postlude to Hindemith's *Ludus Tonalis*, an elaborate fully harmonized palindrome that is musically and intellectually satisfying.

Passacaglia

Originally an early Italian or Spanish dance, its name
being loosely translated as 'streetwalker' (Spanish:
Pasar = to walk, Calle = street). No impropriety is
implied, however; this dance became one of the most
intellectually respectable of musical forms, closely
related to the ground-bass (q.v.). Initially a passacaglia was always in triple time, but Brahms broke this
rule memorably in the finale of the St Antoni variations. This well-known movement will serve as a
useful model, starting as it does with a short phrase
in the bass which by constant repetition and elabo-
ration works its way through increasingly complex
structures until it emerges at the top. *Passacaglia,
Ground,* and *Chaconne* are all close relatives, the
Ground being the most fundamental since it should
properly stay in the bass virtually unaltered, the
Passacaglia being a more liberated version of the
Ground, while the *Chaconne* (also a dance-form in
triple time) reiterates a sequence of harmonies rather
than a melodic phrase. All are severe challenges to
the composer's ingenuity: they represent a narrow
limitation whose disciplines he must respect without
monotony. Probably the two greatest examples are
Bach's Organ Passacaglia in C minor and the last
movement of Brahms's Fourth Symphony.

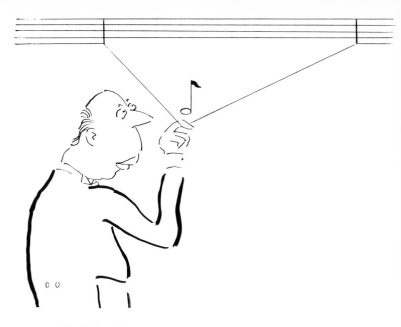

Pedal-point

Organists with big feet are at a disadvantage, and it
is likely that the pedal-point as a composing technique was perforce discovered by an organist whose
left foot became inextricably jammed between E♭
and C♯ while attempting to play a D♮. Snatching
victory from the jaws of disaster, he continued to
improvise heroically above this involuntarily sustained note, thereby astonishing the congregation.
Alternatively it may have originated from one of the
organ's nastiest tricks, known as a 'cipher', when a
note continues to play without human aid, owing to
dirt on the pallet, a rusty pull-down wire, or a weak
pallet-spring—all defects whose only immediate cure

is to pluck out the offending pipe. An organist with great presence of mind might have made a musical virtue out of a cipher by improvising around it while a minion climbed into the works to seek out the persistent note. Whatever its origination, the pedal-point became a respected device, in which the bass note is held for a considerable time while a complex sequence of harmonies is extended above. It was in particular a way of introducing otherwise unacceptable dissonances, which again might originally have expressed the organist's frustration at being unable to get his foot out.

Pentatonic

Extremely economical scale having only five notes, thus simplifying the processes of composition considerably. The child who finds THAT tune on the black notes of the piano is using a pentatonic scale. Much used in Oriental music and folk-songs. It exists in two versions:

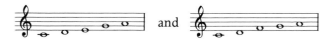 and

Both are liable to induce a certain monotony, but they have proved invaluable in teaching children instrumental music, since if you stick to one or other of the two scales (usually the second) any random combination of sounds will be quite pleasing to the ear, thus avoiding conflict with other members of the school staff.

Pitch

Perfect or *Absolute*   The ability to recognize and identify by name any sound possessing pitch, including even 'abstract' sounds such as the clink of milk-bottles or knocking on wood. One of the more mysterious attributes of the human ear, it has sometimes been described as pitch-memory, since the only rational explanation acceptable to scientists is that the brain has absorbed and registered certain sounds from the earliest years and remembered them accurately. However, there seems to be more to it than that, since there are individuals who possess the ability without having had a musical upbringing. Most musicians have a sense of remembered pitch— if asked to sing a theme from an established work they will do so in approximately the right key. In my own case I 'find' G major by singing the signature tune of 'The Archers' in my mind. The A to which the orchestra tunes is also indelibly impressed on most players' memory. But the possessor of *Absolute Pitch* is capable of absolute accuracy in such matters, and does not need to pause for thought. Of enormous value to singers of avant-garde music, who are expected to pluck notes from the air when surrounded by dissonance, *Absolute Pitch* can be a problem for a singer in more traditional music. If, for example, his colleagues in a choir begin to lose pitch, he will consciously have to sing flat to go with them. A further handicap arrives with advancing age, when the inbuilt pitch seems to sharpen, making all 'heard' music seem out of tune.

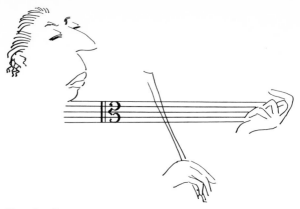

Ponticello

The bridge of a stringed instrument—any stringed instrument: there is no need to say 'pontiviolin' or 'pontidoublebass'. Usually coupled with the word '*sul*'. *Sul ponticello* means that the player should keep the bow close to the little bit of fancy fretwork that supports the strings at their highest point. This produces a curious rustling sort of sound of the chills-run-up-and-down-my-spine variety, much used in background music when villainy is afoot. Done skilfully on purpose it can be very effective; done accidentally by beginners it merely makes Dad wish he'd agreed to buy the little perisher a piano after all.

Prelude

Naturally enough, a prelude would seem to be a piece that precedes something else, often a fugue (q.v.). Like all too many musical terms, though, it has been somewhat loosely used. It can be the opening movement of a dance-suite (the only one not in a dance-form), and thus a sort of warming-up exercise for the performer; it can be the introduction to a song, in which case it's a warming-up period for the singer. Or, and this is quite illogical, it can be a composition complete in itself with no aftermath. Since Bach set a precedent by grouping 24 Preludes and Fugues together, one in each major and minor key, other composers who weren't so hot at counterpoint (q.v.) felt it would make things easier just to write the Preludes on their own while still observing the convention of writing one in each key. Chopin, Rachmaninov, and Scriabin are notable examples of such composers. Surprisingly, though each prelude could be said to lead nowhere (since it's followed by another prelude and then another and then another and then another and then another . . .) the scheme works tolerably well, and is at least considerably more satisfying than a speech consisting of the words 'Ladies and gentlemen' repeated 24 times. However, composers who don't feel up to writing 24 preludes, perhaps because they aren't too sure of how to write some of the more obscure key signatures, may write them one at a time with perfect propriety. Occasionally the term is even used for an orchestral piece, as in Debussy's *Prelude: L'après-midi d'un faune*, which obviously had to stick to being a prelude since Debussy could scarcely describe what *le faune* might have got up to *pendant le soir*.

Quodlibet

(Lat:=whatever you like)   Although the name suggests an academic form of indeterminacy (q.v.) it is properly applied to the musical *jeu d'esprit* in which several tunes are spontaneously and often inappropriately combined. What began as a party game, in which alcohol probably dulled the critical faculty (or some members of it), developed into a sophisticated form of counterpoint. The three dances that Mozart so skilfully combines in *Don Giovanni* are an ingenious example of a *Quodlibet*, as is the combination of themes of widely differing character in the overture to *The Mastersingers*.

Realization

Continuo (q.v.) parts often consist only of a bass line and chord-symbols—a 'figured bass'. To 'realize' a continuo part is to translate the symbols into chords so that the part is fully fleshed. Thus

might be realized as

In printed editions a 'realized' part is often supplied by an editor (*see* EDITING) for the benefit of performers lacking the skill or courage to provide the harmonies themselves. Such parts are often less enterprising than the composers intended them to be and might more properly be described as 'barely realized'.

Rubato

(It. =robbed)   Over the centuries the cry of 'Ancora rubato' (robbed again) has echoed through the corridors of opera-houses as the orchestral musicians opened their pay-packets. In time, the word became so associated with the sight of players hanging about the stage-door waiting to argue with the manager that it seemed natural to apply it to hanging about while playing an expressive melody. It is in fact the subtle art of flexing the rhythm in such a way as to enhance its expressiveness, sometimes retarding, sometimes accelerating, but always preserving a coherent musical shape. Its tasteful use almost invariably depends on an awareness of the relation between a melody and its supporting harmony. Questions of rubato should usually not be worked out but left to the inspiration of the moment. Abused, it can result in gross distortions of the music.

Scordatura

The tuning of a stringed instrument in an abnormal manner for a special effect. Mozart, in his Sinfonia

Concertante for violin and viola, asks the viola player to tune the instrument a semitone higher than usual, so that the written note D sounds E♭, F♯ sounds G, etc. The player's fingers thus play in the relatively easy key of D while sounding in E♭, which could drive you mad if you have perfect pitch. However, the term *scordatura* is more frequently used for aberrations of tuning such as G♯-D-A-E♭ instead of the normal G-D-A-E. This enables the player to find unorthodox chord formations and produce exotic sounds. Bartók does so to brilliant effect in his *Contrasts* for clarinet, violin, and piano where, in one movement, the violinist is required to have two instruments, one tuned normally and one abnormally. A rather similar effect to *scordatura* is produced by most string players in their formative years, the difference being that in their case the only notes *in* tune are the open strings.

Serialism

A method of composing which provides music with a new grammar and syntax to replace tonality (see Atonality for another replacement). Invented by Schoenberg (or, according to Josef Hauer, by Josef Hauer). The system is based on a 'note-row' (pronounced to rhyme with 'No', not 'Now') or 'series' of twelve notes of the chromatic scale, arranged in any order the composer likes so long as each note appears only once. For instance:

According to the rules of the game a composer can use the series either in its Original form, as above; or Inverted, starting with the same note but going up instead of down and vice versa:

or Retrograde, i.e. the Original back to front:

or the Retrograde Inverted, i.e. the Retrograde going

up instead of down, and vice versa:

The intervals between notes 1 and 2 or 4 and 5 may look different to the eye, but are in fact the same in their inverted form.

Having chosen his series and worked out its four forms, as above, the composer sets to work following three basic rules: I. All melodies or fragments of melody must have notes in the same order as one of the four forms. II. All chords must be made up of adjacent notes in one of the four forms. III. Melodies and chords together must work their way through one form of the series before going on to another. It is comforting to realize that the listener is not expected to be able to recognize any of these processes: it is simply a method of working for the composer— sorting himself out, as you might say.

Remember also that a note may be an octave up or down, or two or three octaves up or down, and still be the same note so far as the series is concerned. This helps the composer to break out of what might otherwise be a too rigid straitjacket.

Since statistics prove that there are 479,001,600 possible series, give or take a few, the system isn't all that limiting.

Here is a brief extract from a composer who only wrote rather brief pieces, Webern. The notes in the series are numbered, and we see at play (if that's the word) the Retrograde, the Original, and the Retrograde Inverted, all in four bars:

Series *can* be tonal, with successive notes tracing out tonic and dominant chords and so on. But this is frowned on as not quite proper. They can also sometimes have fewer than twelve notes: Stravinsky's *In memoriam Dylan Thomas* has one of only five. In fact there are all sorts of varieties. For one short period, composers who were determined to show that anything-a-computer-could-do-the-human-brain-could-do-as-badly introduced *Total Serialization*, in which not only pitch but rhythm and dynamics were subject to serial procedures. Like most ultimate solutions it proved to be very temporary.

Sextet

Only included because after that last bit I thought a little sex would be welcome.

Short octave

Only in musical terminology could one find something as totally illogical as this; if the word octave means anything at all it must surely be an interval or range of notes *eight* apart. Actually what we call an octave, A—A, B—B, etc. contains 12 semitones, but since the scales most currently used only involve 8 notes, the term octave is acceptable. What then is a short octave other than one played out of tune? Well, believe it or not, to save expense and presumably space, it was sometimes the custom on organs to have less than a complete octave at the bottom end of the keyboard. Thus one might find the lowest notes to be

It would be hard to imagine anything more calculated to cause an organist to lose his senses, but instead of being called a botchup or a bluddidaft it became known as a short octave.

Supertonic

Gin, Worcester Sauce, and a pinch of bi-carb. Also the second degree of the scale, so called because it is the note above the Tonic (q.v.).

Tessitura

Italian term to describe how the general compass of a piece lies in relation to the voice or instrument for which it is written. Thus a piece for bass consistently using the notes middle C to the F above would have a high tessitura, whereas the same notes for a tenor would have a normal tessitura.

Thumper

Common species of amateur pianist; also a level felt-covered weight placed over the keys of an organ to keep them level, and against which they strike on rising back to the normal position after depression. (The key's depression, not the organist's.)

Tierce de Picardie

A way of cheering everyone up at the end of a sad piece by changing the minor tonality that has prevailed up to now by a major chord in the final bar. Possibly named after Picardie because that's where the roses come from, and a major chord brings a touch of summer. Scarlatti was once heard to remark of Bach, 'Ecco! See 'ow 'ee Picardie major chord for da lasta bar.'

Tierce de Picardie

Tonality

See ATONALITY

Tonic

Usually coupled with gin, but may be drunk 'straight'. The first note of the scale, establishing the tonality (q.v.) of the piece; the key-note. The notes of the normal major scale in ascending order are called Tonic, Supertonic, Mediant, Sub-dominant, Dominant, Sub-mediant, Leading-note, Tonic, an extraordinary collection of names. To use the term 'Sub-mediant' to describe the sixth note of the scale when the third note is called 'Mediant' just shows how tortuously the academic mind works. In this context, 'sub' is supposed to mean less important, but since in 'Sub-dominant' it means 'Below', it can hardly be surprising if students ultimately revolt and riot in the streets!

Transposing instruments

If you look at the key-signatures at the beginning of each page of an orchestral score, you will see that some instruments, such as the cor anglais, clarinets, horns, and trumpets, appear to be playing in a different key from the rest. But with any luck (and provided the player is using the right instrument) they will sound in the *same* key as the rest of the orchestra. The paradox is brought about primarily by mechanical factors. The clarinet, for instance, has a complex system of keys which enable the player to keep his hands in the same position, reaching, by a form of remote control, notes that are outside the normal span of the fingers. However, some do involve extremely awkward fingering. To overcome this, the player has two instruments, the B♭ and the A clarinet.

The written note C

sounds B♮ on the B♭ instrument

and A on the A instrument

In theory this means that the player need never have more than three sharps or flats in the key signature, though, needless to say, skilled players can cope with more and often do. The letter by which a transposing instrument is identified (Trumpets in D, Horns in F, etc.) is always the note that *sounds* from a written C. The ultimate in transpositions is to be found in the saxophone family, in which there are seven instruments, ranging from Sopranino to Contrabass, though these two extreme members are rare. Three consecutive notes written in the treble clef

played in turn on the seven different saxophones would *sound* like this:

This is not quite so insane as it looks, since it means that the same fingering is actually used on all seven instruments, enabling the player to pass from one to the other with perfect facility.

In some scores, notably by a few Soviet composers, all instrumental parts are written 'in C', i.e. non-transposing, but the individual orchestral parts still need to be transposed for the players' benefit.

Tre corde

(It. =three strings)   Most early keyboard instruments such as the spinet or clavichord had a single string to each note. (Why the word 'string' is used to describe a wire remains one of music's mysteries.) Larger instruments such as the harpsichord and even, surprisingly, the earliest pianos of Cristofori had two strings to a note. On the principle that 'more means better', piano manufacturers of the eighteenth century found a way of allotting three strings to the notes in the middle range of the keyboard. This meant that normally the hammer would strike all three strings simultaneously; *tre corde* is therefore only used as a contradiction of *una corda*, meaning 'with one string'. The effect of *una corda* is produced by shifting the hammers to the right so that they strike only one string instead of three, thus producing a softer sound.

The tension sustained by the frame of a large grand is of the order of thirty tons. Part of this tension is relieved by 'cross-stringing' or 'overstringing', distributing the pull of the strings in more than one direction. Pianists however are sometimes even more highly strung than their instruments.

Trio

One of the most potentially confusing words in music since it has (perhaps appropriately) three meanings. (1) a group of three players—fair enough. (2) a composition for a group of three players—also fair enough. But (3) a form, the central section of a Minuet or Scherzo, designed to be a contrast to the preceding section which, *after* the Trio, is then repeated Da Capo (q.v.). Although legend has it that this section was originally played by only three players (hence its name), in practice composers such as Haydn, Mozart, and Beethoven have no hesitation in using more. When the term is also used—as it is— in solo sonatas for piano it becomes even more misleading with its suggestion that another two performers are suddenly called for. The most idiotic use of all occurs in the central section of a march, when the Trio is not even in $\frac{3}{4}$ time.

Tritone

Not a fanfare played on a conch shell by a sea-god in Ancient Times, but the fancy name for the interval (q.v.) of an augmented fourth, so called because it contains three tones.

Its musical significance lies especially in the fact that it represents the two outer poles of tonality, the keys most 'distant' from each other. The key of C has no sharps or flats, the key of F♯ has six sharps, thus cancelling out all the notes of C major save one. It is also the half-way point in the chromatic scale. In early ecclesiastical music it was a forbidden interval and was known as Diabolus in musica, the Devil in music.

Tuning fork

Virtually useless as an eating-tool owing to the bluntness of the prongs and the shortness of the handle, the tuning fork is a metal device which when forcibly struck emits an audible ping. On placing the tip of the handle on to some sort of

tuning fork

resonator (cigar-box, hollow wooden leg, piano sounding-board, etc.) while the upper prongs are still vibrating, a very pure and precise sound will be produced, to which other instruments may then tune. Tuning forks are mostly tuned to A or C, but for medical or acoustic purposes a wider range does exist.

Turn

An ornament in music that circles round a note before coming in to land on it, indicated by the symbol

played thus:

When badly executed, a nasty turn, as when a conductor says to the solo oboist, 'That was a nasty turn you gave me'.

Una corda

If you knew Una like I knew Una you'd refrain from even mentioning her here. But before passions become roused, *see* TRE CORDE.

Urtext

(Ger: =original text)   A vogue word for any edition aspiring to complete authenticity. Since composers often changed their minds and were also liable to human error, an Urtext edition is usually preceded by a lengthy preface in which the editor explains which notes he thinks are absolutely *Ur*, and which are a little *Uh-uh*. Displaying an Urtext edition on the music stand shows you are a cultured musician; following it slavishly shows you are a gullible one.

Violone

At one time or another this word has been used for: a bass viol; any viol; the cello (Handel's usage); a *gross Bassgeiger*; or the double bass. Take your pick. Today it tends to be used for the viol equivalent of the double bass, an octave below the bass viol, but there's nothing compulsory about this.

Vox humana

A reed stop on the organ of very peculiar construction. Nearly always used in conjunction with the tremulant to simulate nervousness or soprano wobble.

Well-tempered

It was generally said by the choristers of St Thomas Kirche, Leipzig that the Cantor's Bach was worse than his Bite. State of mind supposedly rare amongst musicians, but in fact more common than people imagine. It's all to do with having an equal temperament (q.v.).

Whole-tone scale

A six-note scale with no semitones, There are only two such scales since one uses six of the available twelve notes within the octave, the other uses the other six.

Whatever note you begin on you will always end up on one of these two versions of the whole-tone scale, which is perhaps the main reason why it proved to be something of a dead end. Much exploited by Debussy and his imitators, but credit for its invention must be given to Liszt, who uses it with considerable daring in works such as *Unstern*. Whole tone harmonies have a vague and nebulous effect, ideally suited to musical impressionism; having no 'tonic' (q.v.) they are literally rootless.

Xylorimba

A xylophone consists of a number of pieces of wood laid out like a keyboard and having resonators beneath each note to improve the tone-quality. A marimba is similar to a xylophone but is pitched an octave lower. A marimba-xylophone is a xylophone with the extra bottom octave of the marimba added, or a marimba with the extra top octave of a xylophone added, according to your point of view. A xylorimba is a small marimba suitable for percussion students buying instruments by instalments.

Yodel

Exotic form of singing associated with Austrian and Swiss folk-music in which the singer moves rapidly from normal voice to falsetto and back again, like someone in a perpetual state of indecision as to whether he is a baritone or a countertenor. Primarily intended to make the voice carry over long distances, it enabled lonely shepherds to perform duets with colleagues on the other side of a valley. The musical apotheosis of yodelling might be said to have been reached with the duet between oboe and cor anglais in the slow movement of the *Symphonie Fantastique* by Berlioz, and in the Ho-jo-to-ho cries of the Valkyrie.

Zither

Tyrolean instrument such as might have been arrived at by crossing a mandoline with a clavichord. Essentially a flat box containing a sounding-board and with strings drawn across it (as in a clavichord), it is played not with a keyboard but with a plectrum attached to the fingers (as in a mandoline). Popular with tourists.